JN440657

Tales of Great Feats:

Reading and Writing for English Language Learners

Myeong-Hee Seong
Katie Mae Klemsen

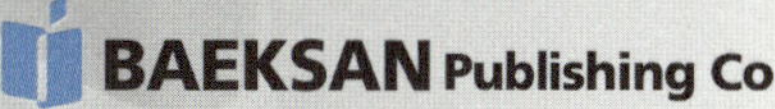

SCOPE AND SEQUENCE

Unit 1

Liz Murray: From Homeless to Harvard

Vocabulary Preview

Create a story using the following words.

homeless	abandon	obstacles
shelter	counsel	inspire
needy	overcome	split

A First Look

1. Read the article below about a famous, inspiring or noteworthy person.

Liz Murray: From Homeless to Harvard

Elizabeth Liz Murray was born September 23, 1980, in the Bronx, New York, to a very poor family. Liz had an extraordinarily difficult childhood. From an early age she and her sister had to learn to care for themselves.

Her education suffered terribly, and she hardly ever attended school. When she was 11, she discovered her mother was HIV positive. After that, Liz's family fell apart. Her parents split up, and her mother moved in with another man, taking Liz's sister with her.

Liz was reluctant to abandon her father, and her relationship with her mother became unfriendly. After a while, she left home and began staying with friends, sleeping on their sofas or floors and then even on the streets.

She became homeless just after she turned 15, when her mother died of AIDS and her father moved to a homeless shelter. Murray's life turned around when she began attending the Humanities Preparatory Academy in Chelsea, Manhattan. Though she started high school later than most students, and did not have a stable home while supporting herself and her sister, Murray graduated in only two years.

She was awarded a New York Times scholarship for needy students and accepted into Harvard University. She entered Harvard in the fall semester of 2000. She left Harvard in 2003 to care for her sick father until 2006 when he died of AIDS. She eventually returned to Harvard in 2006, and graduated in June 2009. As of August 2009, she had begun taking graduate courses at Harvard Summer School and would like to earn a doctorate in clinical psychology to counsel people from all walks of life.

She is the founder and director of Manifest Living, a company that provides a series of workshops that empower adults to create the extraordinary things in their lives. Her life became a movie in 2003, and she now works as a professional speaker, representing the Washington Speakers Bureau. That same strength that pulled her from the streets now inspires others to overcome their own obstacles.

Moral of the story With dedication, desire and effort, anything is possible.

2. Answer each question below. Circle the correct answer.

1) How old was Liz when she became homeless?
   A. 12 years old
   B. 11 years old
   C. 15 years old
   D. Liz was never homeless

2) When did Liz graduate from Harvard?
   A. She graduated in June 2003.
   B. She graduated in June 2009.
   C. She graduated in June 2006.
   D. She will graduate soon.

3) What has Liz's life become?
   A. A movie
   B. A book
   C. A cassette tape
   D. An Mp3 player

4) What would Liz like to do in the future?
   A. She would like to get a doctorate.
   B. She would like to get a doctor.
   C. She would like to walk with people in life.
   D. She would like to become a doctor.

5) What is Manifest Living?
   A. It's a company where Liz works.
   B. It's a company Liz created.
   C. It's a company that helped Liz graduate from Harvard.
   D. It's a company that helps homeless people.

A Closer Look

1. Use the following phrases in complete sentences.

1) care for

____

2) died of

____

3) moved to

____

4) as of

____

5) work as

____

2. Rewrite the words below to form proper and complete sentences. Some sentences can be written more than one way.

1) motivational / is / a / speaker / Liz

Liz ______________________________

2) her / She / when / was / sister / she / cared / young / for

She ______________________________

3) overcome / Her / people / many / will / obstacles / story / help

Her ______________________________

4) in / Harvard / 2009 / graduated / She / from / June

She ______________________________

Looking Back

1. Read the article again. Circle the correct word choice.

Elizabeth Liz Murray **1) was born / is born** September 23, 1980, in the Bronx, New York, to a very poor family. Liz **2) has / had** an extraordinarily difficult childhood. From an early age, she and her sister had to learn to care for **3) themselves / herself**.

Her education suffered terribly, and she hardly ever **4) attending / attended** school. When she was 11, she discovered her mother was HIV positive. After that, Liz's family fell apart. Her parents **5) split / splitted up**, and her mother moved in with another man, **6) took / taking** Liz's sister with her.

Liz was reluctant to abandon her father, and **7) her / his** relationship with her mother became unfriendly. After a while, she left home and began staying with friends, sleeping on **8) their / them** sofas or floors and then even on the streets.

9) Her / She became homeless just after she turned 15, when her mother died of AIDS, and her father moved to a homeless shelter. Murray's life turned around when she began attending the Humanities Preparatory Academy in Chelsea, Manhattan. Though she started high school later than most students, and did not have a stable home while supporting herself and her sister, Murray graduated in only two years.

She was awarded a New York Times scholarship for **10) needy / needing** students and accepted into Harvard University. She entered Harvard in the fall semester of 2000. She left Harvard in 2003 to care for her sick father until 2006 when he died of AIDS. She eventually returned to Harvard in 2006, and graduated in June 2009. As of August 2009, she had begun taking graduate courses at Harvard Summer School and would like to earn a doctorate in clinical psychology to counsel people from all **11) walk / walks** of life.

She is the founder and director of Manifest Living, a company that provides a series of workshops that empower adults to create the extraordinary things in their **12) lives / lifes**. Her life became a movie in 2003 and she now works as a professional speaker, representing the Washington Speakers Bureau. That same strength that pulled her from the streets now inspires others to **13) overcome / overcame** their own obstacles.

Moral of the story With dedication, desire and effort, **14) anything / any thing** is possible.

2. Answer the following questions related to the story.

1) How would you describe Liz's personality? Do you think she is strong? Do you think she is weak? Why?

____

____

____

____

____

2) Why do you think Liz was able to overcome a difficult life and eventually graduate from Harvard?

____

____

____

____

____

3) What does Liz's story teach people about life?

____

____

____

____

____

Last Chance Glance

Read the job profile below.

Counselors

The duties and responsibilities of a counselor vary greatly, depending on their specialty. Counselors usually work with children, teens, adults or families who have problems. Counselors can deal with issues such as mental health disorders, addictions and problems at school.

School Counselors

School counselors provide career and educational counseling. They advocate for students and help them to determine what their talents, interests and abilities are. They also help with career and college information.

Vocational Counselors

Vocational counselors provide career counseling. They help people make career decisions by evaluating peoples' personality, skills, interests and education. They can arrange for aptitude and achievement tests. They also help with job applications.

Rehabilitation Counselors

Rehabilitation counselors help people with physical and emotional disabilities. They arrange for vocational training and job placement. They work with doctors, psychologists and therapists to determine the skills of the client.

Marriage and Family Counselors

Marriage and family counselors try to enhance communication among family members and to prevent crises. They focus on how people relate to each other versus focusing on just one client.

Unit 2

Fauja Singh: The 100-year-old Marathoner

Vocabulary Preview

Create a story using the following words.

marathoner	race	vegetarian
roughly	tracksuit	loser
surgery	competitor	centenarian

A First Look

1. Read the article below about a famous, inspiring or noteworthy person.

Fauja Singh: The 100-year-old Marathoner

It's usually the winner of a race that makes the news, not the loser. But when 100-year-old Fauja Singh crossed the finish line in last position on Sunday, he staggered into the record books as the oldest person to ever finish a marathon. The race was Fauja Singh's eighth marathon. He ran his first at the age of 89. Singh began running roughly 20 years ago after losing his wife and child.

It took the centenarian eight hours to finish the Scotiabank Toronto Waterfront Marathon in Canada, making him the final runner to complete the 42.195 kilometer course and the oldest man in the world to run that far.

Despite his late start to the sport, the Indian runner, who color-coordinated a modern Adidas tracksuit and 'Sikhs in the City' t-shirt with his bright yellow traditional turban, set the 100-meter sprint record for a centenarian before tackling the race.

The Turbaned Tornado says the secret to his success is a life-long vegetarian diet of curry and tea, daily exercise and never smoking or drinking. "I have said it before: that I will carry on running, as it is keeping me alive," Singh said.

It took Singh more than eight hours to cross the finish line of the grueling 42.195 kilometer marathon, long after Kenya's Kenneth Mungara won the event. He has no regrets finishing the race more than six hours after the winner, especially since he is 62 years his senior.

Even though Singh is the oldest man to finish a marathon, the 100-year-old runner has not made it into the Guinness World Records. Guinness spokesman Craig Glenday says his organization won't accept the evidence provided by Fauja that he is actually 100.

Singh, who lives in east London, has a British passport that says he was born in 1911, but holds no birth certificate. His trainer says officials in the part of India where Singh was born didn't issue birth certificates, and Glenday says the man's family might not have registered his birth.

Guinness would accept marriage certificates, military draft details or records of surgery, but the organization didn't see any of those types of documents.

Moral of the story It's never too late to begin something new, better late than never.

2. Answer each question below. Circle the correct answer.

1) How many marathons has Singh completed?
   A. 4 marathons
   B. 18 marathons
   C. 14 marathons
   D. 8 marathons

2) How long did it take for him to finish the marathon?
   A. More than 10 hours
   B. More than 8 hours
   C. More than 6 hours
   D. More than the last marathon he ran

3) Why won't Singh hold the world record?
   A. He did not finish the race.
   B. He lied about his age.
   C. He cannot prove his age.
   D. He is not British.

4) Why does he say he will continue to run?
   A. He will run so he can run faster.
   B. He will run so he can eat the food he likes.
   C. He will run because he doesn't want to smoke.
   D. He will run because it keeps him alive.

5) Which is true about Singh?
   A. He drinks but does not smoke.
   B. He was born in Indonesia.
   C. He is a vegetarian.
   D. He drinks coffee daily.

A Closer Look

1. Use the following phrases in complete sentences.

1) have no regrets

____

2) at the age of

____

3) it took

____

4) it's never too late

____

5) 4 years her senior

____

2. Rewrite the words below to form proper and complete sentences. Some sentences can be written more than one way.

1) hours / finish / the / It / than / took / Singh / line / eight more / cross / to
It ____

2) hours / has / finishing / He / the / no / race / more / winner / than / after / six / regrets
He ____

3) running / about / ago / 20 / Singh / years / started
Singh ____

4) born / cannot / he / when / He / prove / was
He ____

Looking Back

1. Read the article again. Circle the correct word choice.

It's **1) never / usually** the winner of a race that makes the news, not the loser. But when 100-year-old Fauja Singh crossed the finish line in last position on Sunday, **2) she / he** staggered into the record books as the oldest person to ever finish a marathon. The race was Fauja Singh's eighth marathon. He ran his first at the age of 89. Singh **3) began / beginning** running roughly 20 years ago after losing **4) him / his** wife and child.

It **5) took / taked** the centenarian eight hours to finish the Scotiabank Toronto Waterfront Marathon in Canada, making him the final runner to complete the 42.195-kilometer course and the **6) most older / oldest** man in the world to run that far.

Despite his late start to the sport, the **7) indian / Indian** runner, who color-coordinated a modern Adidas tracksuit and 'Sikhs in the City' t-shirt with his bright yellow traditional turban, set the 100-meter sprint record for a centenarian before tackling the race.

The Turbaned Tornado says the secret to his success is a **8) long-life / life-long** vegetarian diet of curry and tea, daily exercise and never smoking or drinking. "I have said it before: that I will carry on running, as it is keeping me alive," Singh said.

It took Singh more than eight hours to cross the finish line of the grueling 42.195 kilometer marathon, long after Kenya's Kenneth Mungara **9) won / winned** the event. He has no regrets finishing the race more than six hours after the winner, especially since he is 62 years his senior.

Even though Singh is the oldest man to finish a marathon, the 100-year-old runner has not made it **10) onto / into** the Guinness World Records. Guinness spokesman

Craig Glenday says his organization won't accept the evidence provided by Fauja that he is actually 100.

Singh, who lives in **11) east / East** London, has a British passport that says he was born in 1911, but holds no birth certificate. His trainer says officials in the part of India where Singh was born didn't issue birth certificates, and Glenday says the man's family might not have registered his birth.

Guinness would accept marriage certificates, military draft details or records of surgery, but the organization didn't see any of those types of documents.

Moral of the story It's never too late to begin something new, better late than never.

2. Answer the following questions related to the story.

1) Why do you think Singh began to run? How has this helped him?

2) Should Singh be honored for this accomplishment? Why or why not?

3) Why do you think it's important to keep trying new things?

Last Chance Glance

Read the job profile below.

Physical Therapist

After running a marathon, becoming injured, or to cure pain caused by disease, you might need to visit a physical therapist. A physical therapist provides services to patients to help improve their mobility, restore physical function and help alleviate pain caused by disease, injury, illness or aging. They work with the patient towards restoring and maintaining their overall health and fitness through therapy.

Physical therapists check the medical history of their patients and then examine and test them to measure their balance, muscle performance, strength, and motor function, range of motion, posture, respiration and coordination. They use these results to come up with a successful treatment strategy so they achieve the desired outcome.

A physical therapist uses electrical stimulation, traction, cold compresses, ultrasound, deep tissue massage and hot packs to reduce swelling and help relieve the patient's pain. They often work with or consult other professional healthcare givers such as physicians, nurses, occupational therapists and audiologists.

Common work activities include:

1. **Meeting with physicians** and treatment teams to understand overall goals for the patient with regards to physical mobility.
2. **Consulting with patients** and performing initial assessments as to the patient's current level of functioning and expectations for the future.
3. **Developing plans** for patients that help increase mobility and ease of movement.
4. **Assisting patients** to learn to use various tools such as walkers, prosthetics, wheelchairs or leg braces.
5. **Using** hot and cold temperature **treatments**, electric stimulation, massage therapy and other treatments to help patients.

Unit 3

Josh Silver: So the World Can See

Vocabulary Preview

Create a story using the following words.

spectacles	sight	physics
colleague	adjust	optician
ambitious	affordable	inventor

A First Look

1. Read the article below about a famous, inspiring or noteworthy person.

Josh Silver: So the World Can See

Josh Silver started his quest on March 23, 1985. He wants to bring sight to a billion people. His quest is to allow the world's poor to see. A professor of physics at Oxford University, Silver was discussing glasses, with a colleague, wondering whether they might be adjusted without the need for expensive specialist equipment, when the light bulb of inspiration first flickered above his head.

What if it were possible, he thought, to make a pair of glasses which, instead of requiring an optician, could be "tuned" by the wearer, to correct his or her own vision? He thought if this were the case, it might be possible to bring affordable glasses to millions of the poorest people in the world that might not otherwise be able to see.

More than two decades after posing that question, Silver now feels he has the answer. The British inventor is breathtakingly ambitious, but he insists his goal is achievable – to offer glasses to a billion of the world's poorest people by 2020. Some 30,000 pairs of the glasses have already been distributed in 15 countries, but to Silver that is not enough. The target, within a few years, is to give away 100 million pairs annually. With the global need for basic sight-correction, by his own detailed research, estimated at more than half the world's population, Silver sees no reason to stop at 1 billion.

Silver has devised a pair of glasses which rely on the principle that the fatter a lens, the more powerful it becomes. Inside the device's tough plastic lenses are two clear circular sacs filled with fluid. Each sac is connected to a small syringe attached to either arm of the glasses.

The wearer adjusts a dial on the syringe to add or reduce the amount of fluid in the membrane, thus changing the power of the lens. When the wearer is happy with the strength of each lens, the membrane is sealed by twisting a small screw, and the syringes are removed. The principle is so simple, the team has discovered, that with very little guidance people are perfectly capable of creating glasses to their own prescription.

"The implications of bringing glasses within the reach of poor communities are enormous," says the scientist. Literacy rates improve greatly; fishermen are able to mend their nets, women to weave clothing. During an early field trial, funded by the British government, in Ghana, Silver met a man called Henry AdjeiMensah, whose sight had deteriorated with age, as all human sight does, and who had been forced to retire as a tailor because he could no longer see to thread the needle of his sewing machine. "So he retired. He was about 35. He could have worked for at least another 20 years. We put these glasses on him, and he smiled, and threaded his needle. He can work now. He can see."

Making and distributing a billion pairs of spectacles is no small task, of course – even at a dollar each (the target cost), and without Silver taking any profit, the cost is huge. This is what Silver calls "the challenge of scaling up".

Silver says, "Things are never simple. But I will solve this problem if I can. And I won't really let people stand in my way."

Moral of the story One person can make a difference in the lives of many.

A Zulu man, wearing a pair of Silver's glasses

A center in Africa where Josh Silver's glasses are being distributed

2. Answer each question below. Circle the correct answer.

1) When did Josh Silver begin his quest to bring sight to poor people?
   A. March 23, 2020
   B. March 23, 1958
   C. March 23, 1985
   D. He will begin his project next year.

2) What is Josh Silver's primary job?
   A. He is an optician.
   B. He is a professor at Harvard.
   C. He only works on this project.
   D. He is a professor at Oxford.

3) How many people does Josh Silver want to help?
   A. 30,000
   B. 1 million
   C. 1 billion
   D. 100,000

4) Why do Silver's glasses work in the developing world?
   A. They are easy to ship.
   B. They are not free.
   C. They are disposable.
   D. They do not require an expert.

5) What is not a benefit of the self-adjusting glasses?
   A. Men can fix holes in fishing nets.
   B. More people will learn to read.
   C. Silver can make a lot of money.
   D. Women can weave fabric.

A Closer Look

1. Use the following phrases in complete sentences.

1) people are perfectly capable of

____

2) What if

____

3) attached to

____

4) no longer

____

5) make a difference

____

2. Rewrite the words below to form proper and complete sentences. Some sentences can be written more than one way.

1) bring / billion / He / people / to / sight / to / a / wants

He ____

2) not / glasses / The / require / equipment / do / special

The glasses ____

3) devised / a / of / Silver / pair / has / glasses

Silver ____

4) We / on / put / him / these / glasses

We ____

Looking Back

1. Read the article again. Circle the correct word choice.

Josh Silver started his quest on March 23, 1985. He wants to bring sight to a billion people. His quest is to **1) allowing / allow** the world's poor to see. A professor of **2) Physics / physics** at Oxford University, Silver was discussing glasses with a colleague, wondering whether they might be adjusted without the need for expensive specialist **3) equipments / equipment**, when the light bulb of inspiration first flickered above his head.

What if it were possible, he thought, to make a pair of glasses which, instead of requiring an optician, could be "tuned" by the wearer, to correct **4) their / his or her** own vision? He thought if this were the case, it might be possible to bring affordable glasses to millions of the **5) most poor / poorest** people in the world that might not **6) otherwise / other wise** be able to see.

More than two decades after posing that question, Silver now feels he has the answer. The British inventor is breathtakingly ambitious, but he insists his goal is achievable – to offer glasses to a billion of the world's poorest people by 2020. Some 30,000 pairs of the glasses have already been distributed in 15 countries, but to Silver that is not enough. The target, within a few years, is to give away 100 million pairs annually. With the global need for basic sight-correction, by his own detailed research, estimated at more than half the world's population, Silver sees no reason to stop at 1 billion.

Silver **7) has / had** devised a pair of glasses, which rely on the principle that the fatter a lens, the more powerful it becomes. Inside the device's tough plastic lenses are two clear circular sacs filled with fluid. Each sac is connected to **8) the / a** small syringe attached to either arm of the glasses.

The wearer **9) adjusts / adjusting** a dial on the syringe to add or reduce the amount of fluid in the membrane, thus changing the power of the lens. When the wearer is happy with the strength of each lens, the membrane is sealed by twisting a small screw, and the syringes are removed. The **10) principal / principle** is so simple, the team has discovered, that with very little guidance people are perfectly capable of creating glasses to their own prescription.

11) "**An / The** implications of bringing glasses within the reach of poor communities are enormous," says the scientist. Literacy rates improve greatly; fishermen are able to mend their nets, women to weave clothing. During an early field trial, funded by the British government, in Ghana, Silver **12) meet / met** a man called Henry Adjei-Mensah, whose sight had deteriorated with age, as all human sight does, and who had been forced to retire as a tailor because he could no longer see to thread the needle of his sewing machine. Silver said, "So, he retired. He was about 35. He could have worked for at least another 20 years. We put these glasses on him, and he smiled, and **13) threaded / thread** his needle. He can work now. He can see."

Making and distributing a billion pairs of spectacles is no small task, of course – even at a dollar each (the target cost), and without Silver taking **14) none / any** profit, the cost is staggering. This is what Silver calls "the challenge **15) is scaling up / of scaling up**".

Silver says, "Things are never simple. But I will solve this problem if I can. And I won't really let people stand in my way."

Moral of the story One person can make a difference in the lives of many.

2. Answer the following questions related to the story.

1) How can bringing affordable, easy-to-use glasses to a billion poor people help the world? How can this impact your own country?

____

____

____

____

____

2) What does Silver mean when he talks about 'the challenge of scaling up'?

____

____

____

____

____

3) If you could bring one benefit to humanity, what would you do? Why is this important to you? How would it change the world?

____

____

____

____

____

Last Chance Glance

Read the job profile below.

Optometrists

Optometrists examine eyes and treat vision problems, usually by prescribing eyeglasses or contact lenses, vision therapy, or rehabilitation programs. They also prescribe medicines to treat some eye diseases and allergies.

Optometrists examine patients' eyes with several instruments. Retinoscopes, for example, help them see how patients react to lenses of different strengths. Ophthal-moscopes allow them to see the inside of the eye. Based on their examinations, they make diagnoses, such as nearsightedness or farsightedness, and prescribe lenses or other treatments. If they diagnose eye diseases that need surgery, they refer patients to ophthalmologists (physicians who perform eye surgery). Sometimes optometrists discover eye conditions caused by systemic problems, such as diabetes or high blood pressure, and refer their patients to other medical doctors.

Most optometrists have their own practices or are associates in group practices. Others are employed in hospitals, clinics, and health or government agencies. Still others work for insurance companies; for manufacturers of eyeglasses, contact lenses, and other optical equipment; or for large eyewear chains. Some jobs involve the designing and testing of new products.

Unit 4

Clara Barton: Breaking Boundaries for Women and Nurses

Vocabulary Preview

Create a story using the following words.

battlefield	front	dedicate
decline	first-hand	alter
exclusively	horror	assistance

A First Look

1. Read the article below about a famous, inspiring or noteworthy person.

Clara Barton: Breaking Boundaries for Women and Nurses

Clara, born on Christmas day 1821, was the daughter of Captain Stephen and Sarah Barton. Her father was a respected farmer, horse breeder and politician. Because she was the youngest of five children, most of her education came from her two brothers and two sisters. Although a shy child, she accelerated early in her studies. By the time she was 4 years old, Clara could easily spell complicated words. Her instinctual gift of nursing started at the young age of 11, when she nursed her brother David through a serious illness.

Clara Barton became a teacher in Massachusetts at the age of 17, founded her own school six years later and after ten years of teaching, felt the need to alter her career path. She then studied writing and languages at the Liberal Institute in Clinton, New York.

Following these studies, Barton opened a free school in New Jersey. The attendance, under her leadership, grew to 600, but instead of hiring Barton to head the school, the board hired a man. Frustrated, she moved to Washington D.C. and began work as a clerk in the U.S. Patent Office; this was the first time a woman had received a substantial clerkship in the federal government of the United States.

With the emergence of the US Civil War, Barton refused to take a salary from the government's treasury and dedicated herself to aiding soldiers on the front. Never before had women been allowed in hospitals, camps or on battlefields; initially, military and civil officials declined her help. Eventually, she gained the trust of these officials and began receiving supplies from all over the country. As a result of her untiring work, she became known as the "Angel of the Battlefield." Officially, she became the superintendent of Union nurses in 1864, and began obtaining camp and hospital supplies, assistants and military trains for her work on the front. She practiced nursing exclusively on battlefields, experiencing first-hand the horrors of war on sixteen different battlefields.

Barton was the President of the American National Red Cross for twenty-two years. Under her leadership, she adapted the frame-work of the Red Cross to fit the needs of the United States not only during wartime, but also in peacetime.

Internationally, countries noticed and recognized the need for such peacetime assistance, and in 1884 the Geneva Convention passed the "American Amendment" to include this concept.

Barton was the most decorated American woman, receiving the Iron Cross, the Cross of Imperial Russia and the International Red Cross Medal. Her final act was founding the National First Aid Society in 1904. She retired as President of the American Red Cross at the age of 83 and spent her remaining years in Glen Echo, Maryland where she died from complications of a cold.

Moral of the story Well-behaved women rarely make history.

2. Answer each question below. Circle the correct answer.

1) When was Clara born?

A. December 24, 1921

B. December 24, 1821

C. December 25, 1821

D. There is no date given in the story.

2) Which statement is not true?

A. Clara received many awards.

B. Clara died of a cold.

C. Clara founded the American Red Cross

D. Clara worked in a hospital.

3) Why was being a battlefield nurse difficult?

A. Women were not usually allowed in battle.

B. The military officials did not initially trust her.

C. It was a dirty and dangerous job.

D. Sexism was an issue in the United States at the time.

4) What was her final act?

A. She founded the American Red Cross.

B. She founded a hospital.

C. She founded the National First Aid Society.

D. She founded the first national aid society.

5) How many different battlefields did Clara work on as a nurse?

A. 61

B. 160

C. 600

D. 16

A Closer Look

1. Use the following phrases in complete sentences.

1) experience first-hand

____

2) as a result of

____

3) recognized the need for

____

4) he / she became known as

____

5) with the emergence of

____

2. Rewrite the words below to form proper and complete sentences. Some sentences can be written more than one way.

1) on / first / Clara / battlefield / women / the / the / was

Clara ____

2) a / 17 / teacher / the / age / at / of / became / She

She ____

3) Clara / spell / could / words / complicated / easily

Clara ____

4) She / complications / a / cold / of / from / died

She ____

Looking Back

1. Read the article again. Circle the correct word choice.

Clara, born on Christmas **1) Day / day** 1821, was the daughter of Captain Stephen and Sarah Barton. Her father was a respected farmer, horse breeder and politician. Because she was the youngest of five children, most of her education came from her two brothers and two sisters. Although a shy child, she accelerated early in her studies. By the time she was 4 years old, Clara could easily spell complicated words. Her instinctual gift of nursing started at the young age of 11, when she nursed her brother David through a **2) serious / seriousness** illness.

Clara Barton became a teacher in Massachusetts at the age of 17; **3) found / founded** her own school six years later, and after ten years of teaching, felt the need to **4) alter / antler** her **5) carrier / career** path. She then **6) studied / studyed** writing and languages at the Liberal Institute in Clinton, New York.

Following these studies, Barton opened a free school in New Jersey. The attendance, **7) on / under 8) she / her** leadership, grew to 600, but instead of hiring Barton to head the school, the board hired a man. Frustrated, she moved to Washington D.C. and began work as a clerk in the U.S. Patent Office; this was the first time **9) the / a** woman had received a substantial clerkship **10) from / in** the federal government of the United States.

11) With / because the emergence **12) of / about** the **US** Civil War, Barton refused to take **13) a / the** salary from the government's treasury and dedicated herself to aiding soldiers on the front. Never before had women been allowed **14) on / in** hospitals, camps or on battlefields; initially, military and civil officials declined her help. Eventually, she gained the trust of these officials and began receiving supplies from all over the country. As a result of her untiring work, she became known **15) by / as** the "Angel of the Battlefield." Officially, she became the superintendent of Union nurses in 1864, and began obtaining camp and hospital supplies, assistants and military trains for her work on the front. She practiced nursing exclusively on battlefields, experiencing first-hand the horrors of war on sixteen different battlefields.

Barton was the President of the American National Red Cross for twenty-two years. Under her leadership, she adapted the framework of the Red Cross to fit the needs of the United States not only during wartime, but also in peacetime.

Internationally, countries noticed and recognized the need for such peacetime assistance, and in 1884 the Geneva Convention passed the "American Amendment" to include this concept.

Barton was the most decorated American woman, receiving the Iron Cross, the Cross of Imperial Russia and the International Red Cross Medal. Her final act was founding the National First Aid Society in 1904. She retired as President of the American Red Cross at the age of 83 and spent her remaining years in Glen Echo, Maryland where she died from complications of a cold.

Moral of the story Well-behaved women rarely make history.

2. Answer the following questions related to the story.

1) Describe the type of personality you think Clara might have had, and explain your answer. (Use adjectives!)

____

____

____

____

____

2) Why do you think Clara chose nursing as a profession?

____

____

____

____

____

3) In your opinion, was it foolish of Clara to go to battlefields to perform her nursing duties?

____

____

____

____

____

Last Chance Glance

Read the job profile below.

Nurses

Adult nurses care for adult patients who are suffering from acute and long-term illnesses and diseases. They support recovery from illness or operation by using care plans, carrying out care procedures and assessments and by focusing on the needs of the patient rather than the illness or condition. They also promote good health and well-being through education.

Nurses usually work within a multidisciplinary team but are the main point of contact for patients, often providing the greatest continuity of care. Adult nurses work mainly in hospitals and the community, attached to a health center or general practice and in residential homes, specialist units, schools and hospices. Many nurses work with patients in their own homes.

Typical work activities

Gaining the trust and confidence of each patient is an important aspect of the job for nurses, especially as they have more contact with the patients than other members of the medical team. This extends to developing a good relationship with the patient's relatives as well, particularly in cases of chronic illness where the patient may be returning regularly for treatment.

The Western trend for community-based care has led to an increase in the number of opportunities for working in the community. It is possible for a newly qualified nurse to work in the community, although many gain a year's hospital experience first. These nurses often visit patients' homes and provide care on-site.

Exact duties may vary depending on the country where a nurse is working.

Unit 5

Taylor Mali: What a Teacher Makes

Vocabulary Preview

Create a story using the following words.

advocate	author	poetry
passionate	viral	famous
courage	persuasion	draft

A First Look

1. Read the article below about a famous, inspiring or noteworthy person.

Taylor Mali: What a Teacher Makes

Born in New York City in 1965, Taylor Mali is a vocal advocate of teachers and the nobility of teaching, having spent nine years in the classroom himself as a teacher. He taught everything from English and history to math and S.A.T. test preparation. He has performed and lectured for teachers all over the world, and he had a goal of creating 1,000 new teachers through "poetry, persuasion, and perseverance."

He became an Internet sensation when a performance of his went viral. It was a passionate, persuasive story of a conversation he had with his friends. One day at dinner, a friend of his, who was a lawyer, asked him, "Taylor, what do you make?" This question is essentially asking how much money he earns. Taylor was shocked, but not angry. Instead of getting angry, he got motivated to teach his friends about what a teacher makes. The following is a selection from his famous speech:

You want to know what I make?

I make kids work harder than they ever thought they could. I can make a C+ feel like a Congressional medal of honor, and an A- feel like a slap in the face.

I make kids sit through 40 minutes of study hall in absolute silence. No, you may not work in groups. No, you may not ask a question. Why won't I let you get a drink of water? Because you're not thirsty; you're bored, that's why.

I make parents tremble in fear when I call home: I hope I haven't called at a bad time, I just wanted to talk to you about something Billy said today. Billy said, "Leave the kid alone. I still cry sometimes, don't you?" And it was the noblest act of courage I have ever seen.

I make parents see their children for who they are and what they can be.

You want to know what I make?

I make kids wonder, I make them question. I make them criticize. I make them apologize and mean it. I make them write, write, write; and then I make them read. I make them spell "definitely beautiful," "definitely beautiful," "definitely beautiful," over and over and over again, until they will never misspell either one of those words again. I make them show all their work in math; and hide it on their final drafts in English.

Let me break it down for you, so you know what I say is true: I make a goddamn difference! What about you?

Mali is the author of two books of poetry, and four CDs of spoken word. He received a New York Foundation for the Arts Grant in 2001 to develop *Teacher! Teacher!* a one-man show about poetry, teaching, and math, which won the jury prize for best solo performance at the 2001 Comedy Arts Festival. He now earns a living as a poet.

Moral of the story If you love what you do, you'll never go to "work" a day in your life.

2. Answer each question below. Circle the correct answer.

1) What is Taylor's job now?
   A. Teacher
   B. Actor
   C. Poet
   D. Author

2) Which statement is not true?
   A. Mali is an advocate of teachers.
   B. Mali was a teacher for 8 years.
   C. Mali is a poet and spoken word artist.
   D. Mali is angry with his friends.

3) What was he trying to teach his friends at dinner?
   A. That there should be 1,000 new teachers.
   B. The most important part of teaching is not the salary.
   C. Teachers make enough money.
   D. Teaching is a hard job.

4) How did Mali become famous?
   A. He got a virus and it was posted on the Internet.
   B. His performance went viral on the Internet.
   C. He won a prize.
   D. That information is not provided.

5) Which goal does Taylor Mali have?
   A. To inspire 1,000 people to become teachers
   B. To employ 1,000 teachers
   C. To create 1,000 presentations about teaching
   D. To persuade his friends to respect teachers

A Closer Look

1. Use the following phrases in complete sentences.

1) you want to know

____

2) instead of

____

3) in fear

____

4) in absolute silence

____

5) the nobility of

____

2. Rewrite the words below to form proper and complete sentences. Some sentences can be written more than one way.

1) teachers / Taylor / is / of / an / advocate
Taylor ____

2) as / the / a / He / profession / of / promotes / teaching / nobility
He ____

3) Mali / of / author / two / is / the / books
Mali ____

4) now / living / poet / as / a / a / earns / He
He ____

Looking Back

1. Read the article again. Circle the correct word choice.

Taylor Mali: What a Teacher Makes

Born **1) in / at** New York City in 1965, Taylor Mali is a vocal advocate of teachers and **2) the / a** nobility of teaching, having spent nine years **3) in the / at the** classroom himself, as a teacher. He taught everything from English and history to math and S.A.T. test preparation. He has performed and **4) lectured / lecturing** for teachers all over the world, and he has a goal of creating 1,000 new teachers **5) thorough / through** "poetry, persuasion, and perseverance."

He became an Internet sensation when a performance of his went viral. It was a passionate, persuasive story of a conversation he had with **6) he's / his** friends. One day at dinner, a friend of his, who was a lawyer, asked him, "Taylor, what do you make?" This question is essentially asking how much money he earns. Taylor was shocked, but not angry. Instead of getting angry, he got motivated to teach his friends about what a teacher makes. The following is a selection from his famous speech:

> You want to know what I make?
>
> I make kids work harder than they ever thought they could. I can make a C+ feel like a Congressional medal of honor, and an A- feel like a slap in the face.
>
> I make kids sit through 40 minutes of study hall in absolute silence. No, you may not work in groups. No, you may not ask a question. Why won't I let you get a drink of water? Because you're not thirsty; you're bored, that's why.
>
> I make parents tremble in fear when I call home: I hope I haven't called at a bad time, I just wanted to talk to you about something Billy said today. Billy said, "Leave the kid alone. I still cry sometimes, don't you?"

And it was *7) the noblest / the most noble* act of courage I have ever seen.

I make parents see their children for *8) whom / who* they are, and what they can be.

You want to know what I make?

I make kids wonder, I make them question. I make them criticize. I make them apologize and mean it. I make them write, write, write; and then I make them read. I make them spell "definitely beautiful," "definitely beautiful," "definitely beautiful," over and over and over again, until they will never misspell *9) either / neither* one of those words again. I make them show all their work in math; and hide it *10) in / on* their final drafts in English.

Let me break it down for you, so you know what I say is true: I make a goddamn difference! What about you?

Mali is the author of two books of poetry, and four CDs of spoken word. He received a New York Foundation for the Arts Grant in 2001 to develop *Teacher! Teacher!* a one-man show about poetry, teaching, and math, which won the jury prize for best solo performance at the 2001 Comedy Arts Festival. He now earns a living as a poet.

Moral of the story If you love what you do, you'll never go to "work" a day in your life.

2. Answer the following questions related to the story.

1) Do you think teaching is a noble profession? Why? Why not?

____

____

____

____

____

2) What does the title of this article, "What a Teacher Makes" mean?

____

____

____

____

____

3) What was the message Taylor Mali was trying to teach his friends that night at dinner?

____

____

____

____

____

Last Chance Glance

Read the job profile below.

Teachers

Teachers teach children to read, write, do math, and much more. They use games, videos, computers, and other tools to teach children different subjects. They show students skills. They also explain information. Teachers plan their lessons before they teach, which can take a lot of time.

Teachers try to make their lessons easy to understand. They teach things in different ways so that different students can learn in the way that is best for them. Teachers might use a chalkboard, a projector, or a computer. They make handouts or worksheets before class starts. Teachers plan the schedule for the day. Teachers also assign homework and class projects. They often have students work together to do projects.

After class, teachers grade papers and projects. They also create tests. They write students' report cards, and they meet with parents to try to help their children do better in school. Teachers sometimes go to workshops to learn how to teach better. Some teachers also help with sports or other after-school activities.

Most kindergarten and elementary school teachers teach several subjects to one class. In some schools, two or more teachers work as a team. Other teachers teach one special subject, such as art, music, reading, or physical education.

Most middle school and high school teachers focus on one subject. They might teach English, science, or history, for example. Some teach students how to do a job. High school teachers spend more time explaining a subject and less time with activities like games.

All teachers in public schools must have a teaching certificate and a license to teach. You must have a college degree to be a teacher. You must take classes in education and practice teaching with the help of an experienced teacher.

Unit 6

Angela Zhang: 17 Year-old Could Cure Cancer

Vocabulary Preview

Create a story using the following words.

particle	tumor	treatment
initiative	mentor	creativity
eradicate	trigger	cause

A First Look

1. Read the article below about a famous, inspiring or noteworthy person.

Angela Zhang: 17 Year-old Could Cure Cancer

Angela Zhang, 17, a high school student from Cupertino, Calif., won a $100,000 scholarship from the Siemens Foundation for research that created a tiny particle she likened to a "Swiss army knife of cancer treatments" because of its precision in targeting cancer tumors - setting the world record for the Youngest Cancer Researcher, according to the World Records Academy

The winners announced Monday had competed against 2,436 fellow students who submitted 1,541 projects to the 2011 Siemens Competition in Math, Science & Technology. Angela Zhang, a senior at Monta Vista High School in Cupertino, California, won the $100,000 Grand Prize in the individual category for using nanotechnology to eradicate cancer stem cells. I asked, 'Why does this happen. Why does cancer cause death? What are we doing to fix this and what can I do to help,' said the Monta Vista High School senior.

Zhang said the particle she designed improves on current cancer treatments because it delivers a drug directly to tumor cells and doesn't affect healthy cells around it. The particle is also able to release a drug when activated by a laser.

The idea is still years away from being used in patients, however. Zhang says it could take 25 years between clinical trials and other steps before her research is helping patients.

Angela won the Intel International Science & Engineering Fair (ISEF) Grand Award for medicine and health science in 2010 and 2011.

She is a 2010 Siemens Competition Regional Finalist who began her work on this project in 2009 and spent an estimated 1,000 hours on her research. Angela hopes to become a research professor. Her mentor was Dr. Zhen Cheng of Stanford University.

She plays golf and the piano and would like to major in chemical or biomedical engineering or physics. "Angela created a nanoparticle that is like a Swiss army knife of cancer treatment," said competition judge Dr. Tejal Desai, Professor, Department of Bioengineering and Therapeutic Sciences, University of California, San Francisco. "She showed great creativity and initiative in designing a nanoparticle system that can be triggered to release drugs at the site of the tumor while also allowing for non-invasive imaging. Her work is an important step in developing new approaches to the therapeutic targeting of tumors via nanotechnology."

Moral of the story Young people can make important contributions to science, technology and society.

2. Answer each question below. Circle the correct answer.

1) How many students competed in the competition?

A. 100,000
B. 1,541
C. 2,436
D. 2,010

2) Why is Angela's research an improvement on current cancer research?

A. It uses lasers to kill cancer cells.
B. It is available to patients now.
C. It uses drugs to kill the cancer cells.
D. It targets tumors, and not healthy cells.

3) What does Angela dream of becoming?

A. She would like to become a research professor.
B. She would like to become a teaching professor.
C. She would like to become a doctor.
D. She would like to fight cancer.

4) Which statement is not true about Angela?

A. She won $100,000.
B. She is a high school junior.
C. She developed a particle that fights cancer.
D. The particle she developed uses nanotechnology.

5) Why did Angela want to research cancer-fighting particles?

A. She wanted to understand why cancer kills people.
B. Her mother died of cancer.
C. She wanted to win $100,000.
D. She wants to be a famous researcher.

A Closer Look

1. Use the following phrases in complete sentences.

1) show great creativity

____

2) what can I do to

____

3) because of

____

4) is able to

____

5) major in

____

2. Rewrite the words below to form proper and complete sentences. Some sentences can be written more than one way.

1) Why / cause / does / death / cancer / ?
Why ______________________________

2) youngest / She / the / the / cancer / world / researcher / in / is
She ______________________________

3) She / creativity / showed / great / designing / in / a / nanoparticle / system
She ______________________________

4) Angela / Grand / for / Prize / medicine / won / the
Angela ______________________________

Looking Back

1. Read the article again. Circle the correct word choice.

Angela Zhang, 17, **1) the / a** high school student from Cupertino, Calif., won **2) the / a** $100,000 scholarship from **3) the / a** Siemens Foundation for research that created a tiny particle she likened to a "Swiss army knife of cancer treatments" because of its precision in targeting cancer tumors – setting the world record for the Youngest Cancer Researcher, according **4) to / by** the World Records Academy

The winners announced Monday **5) have / had** competed against 2,436 fellow students **6) who / whom** submitted 1,541 projects to the 2011 Siemens Competition in Math, Science & Technology. Angela Zhang, **7) the / a** senior **8) at / in** Monta Vista High School in Cupertino, California, won the $100,000 Grand Prize in the Individual category for **9) using / used** nanotechnology to eradicate cancer stem cells. "I asked, 'Why does this happen. Why does cancer cause death? What are we doing to fix this and what can I do to help,'" said the Monta Vista **10) high school / High School** senior.

Zhang said the particle she designed improves on current cancer treatments because it delivers a drug directly to tumor cells and doesn't affect healthy cells around it. The particle is also able to release a drug when activated by a laser.

The idea is still years away from being used in patients, however. Zhang says it could take 25 years between clinical trials and other steps before her research is helping patients.

Angela **11) wined / won** the Intel International Science & Engineering Fair (ISEF) Grand Award for medicine and health science in 2011 and 2010.

She is a 2010 Siemens Competition Regional Finalist who began her work on this project **12) in / on** 2009 and spent **13) a / an** estimated 1,000 hours on her research. Angela hopes to become a research professor. Her mentor was Dr. Zhen Cheng of Stanford University.

She plays golf and the piano and would like to major in chemical or biomedical engineering or physics. "Angela created a nanoparticle that is like a Swiss army knife of cancer treatment," said competition judge Dr. Tejal Desai, Professor, Department of Bioengineering and Therapeutic Sciences, University of California, San Francisco. "She showed great creativity and initiative in designing a nano-particle system that can be triggered to release drugs at the site of the tumor while also **14) allowing / allows** for non-invasive imaging. Her work is an important step in developing new **15) approached / approaches** to the therapeutic targeting of tumors via nanotechnology."

Moral of the story Young people can make important contributions to science, technology and society.

2. Answer the following questions related to the story.

1) Do you think young people can make as important discoveries as adults in the fields of technology and science? Why or why not?

____
____
____
____
____

2) Do you think Angela is an ordinary teenager? Why or why not? Can ordinary teenagers make a difference in general society? What kind of difference can they make?

____
____
____
____
____

3) What do you dream of doing? What kind of important contribution would you like to make to the field of science or technology, or to society in general?

____
____
____
____
____

Last Chance Glance

Read the job profile below.

Biomedical Engineer

Biomedical Engineering is the application of engineering principles and design concepts to medicine and biology. This field seeks to close the gap between engineering and medicine. It combines the design and problem solving skills of engineering with medical and biological sciences to improve healthcare diagnosis, monitoring and therapy.

Biomedical engineering has only recently emerged as its own discipline, compared to many other engineering fields. Such an evolution is common as a new field transition from being an interdisciplinary specialization among already-established fields, to being considered a field in itself. Much of the work in biomedical engineering consists of research and development, spanning a broad array of subfields.

No single occupation is expected to have more job growth over the next decade or so. Employment of biomedical engineers is expected to grow by a whopping 72 percent — adding nearly 12,000 jobs — between 2008 and 2018, according to the US Labor Department. The anticipated growth results from the aging generations, and corresponding increase in the need for medical procedures, along with the appetite for medical innovation and advancement.

"Median yearly wages for biomedical engineers were $78,860 in 2009," the US Labor Department reports. The highest-paid 10 percent make more than $123,000, while the lowest-paid 10 percent make less than $50,000. Currency is in United States dollars.

Unit 7

Jordan Romero: To the Top of the World

Vocabulary Preview

Create a story using the following words.

summit	snowstorm	avalanche
overlook	conquer	ascend
backpack	ridge	peak

A First Look

1. Read the article below about a famous, inspiring or noteworthy person.

Jordan Romero: To the Top of the World

On Christmas Eve 2011, a 15-year-old from California phoned his mother to tell her where he was. He was on the summit of Mount Vinson, overlooking the Ronne Ice Shelf, about 1,200km from the South Pole.

At her home in the town of Big Bear, Leigh Anne Drake has received calls, from six similarly elevated locations, in the past five years. At the age of ten, her son had been on the summit of Mount Kilimanjaro. Over the course of 2007, he was on top of Mount Kosciuszko in Australia, Mount Elbrus in Russia and Mount Aconcagua in Argentina. The following year, he ticked off America's Mount McKinley. In 2009, he was on the Carstensz Pyramid in Indonesia.

Last year not long before he graduated from junior high school, Jordan Romero had called his mother to tell her he had become the youngest climber to reach the top of Mount Everest, at the age of 13. Now, he has called to say that he was the youngest person to have conquered the seven highest summits on each of the seven continents, as well as climbing Mount Kosciuszko.

"Team Jordan" had set off up their final peak in a snowstorm on Tuesday. On Friday, they ascended a high ridge in bright sunshine and reached the summit shortly before 1 pm, Antarctic time. "I'm the proudest dad in the world right now," said Paul Romero, who has accompanied and chivvied his son to the top of all seven peaks, along with his wife, Karen Lundgren, Jordan Romero's stepmother.

Mr. Romero, an air ambulance paramedic, who may also be due recognition as the world's most competitive father, began preparing his son for these feats after the nine-year-old Jordan pointed to a mural depicting the seven summits, on a wall in his primary school. He said: "Hey dad, I want to climb these mountains." Jordan's father was eager to support his son, and also thought the idea of summiting the peaks sounded like a great adventure.

He was also keen to do it while he was still in his early forties and physically capable of the challenge. He said: "Well then, we'd better start training." Jordan duly commenced five years of runs, carrying weighted backpacks, and nights spent sleeping in a hypoxic tent, to become accustomed to the thin mountaintop air. "As soon as the sun wakes up, we make waffles, burn down a couple of cups of coffee and just go hard until dark," Mr. Romero told *The Times* last year. "We've redefined family quality time."

Mr. Romero has occasionally faced criticism for pushing Jordan too hard, too young, particularly after another precocious Californian, Abby Sunderland, 16, had to be rescued while attempting to sail solo around the globe. Mr. Romero defended his vigorous style of parenting by pointing to the unhealthy lifestyles that other parents allowed their children to lead. Jordan at least, was never likely to get fat.

I'd say 'I don't even want to smell a bad attitude today,' Mr. Romero said, recalling their hike up to Everest Base Camp. "If that didn't work, it would be, 'OK, drop and give me 40 pushups.' It's amazing what doing 40 push-ups does for your attitude."

Further up Everest, Jordan, his father and stepmother were engulfed in an avalanche that killed a fellow climber and dragged them down the mountainside towards a crevasse.

"We jokingly told Jordan that he couldn't tell his mom about it until he was 18," said Ms. Lundgren.

Yesterday, Ms. Drake would have been pleased to learn that her son was safely back at the base camp beneath Mount Vinson Massif, and preparing to return to

California to thank his sponsors, offer his services as a motivational speaker and catch up on his homework.

Moral of the story Know no limits.

2. Answer each question below. Circle the correct answer.

1) How many mountains has Jordan climbed?
   A. Seven
   B. Eight
   C. One
   D. This information is not provided.

2) What do critics say about Jordan's father?
   A. They say he is great for pushing his son.
   B. They say he is a bad father.
   C. They worry that he pushes his son too hard.
   D. They say Jordan is a lot like his father, and both are too competitive.

3) What is Jordan's next plan?
   A. He wants to continue hiking and climbing.
   B. He wants to be a motivational speaker.
   C. He wants to write a book.
   D. He wants to catch up on his homework.

4) How did Jordan begin his training?
   A. He ran with a weighted backpack.
   B. He did 40 push-ups.
   C. He studied hard.
   D. He went to bed early.

5) What happened on Christmas Eve, 2011?
   A. Jordan Romero made a world record.
   B. Jordan Romero finished the 7 Summits challenge.
   C. Jordan Romero became the youngest person to climb Mount Vinson.
   D. All of the above are true.

A Closer Look

1. Use the following phrases in complete sentences.

1) not long before

____

2) pleased to learn that

____

3) was keen to

____

4) sounded like

____

5) was never likely to

____

2. Rewrite the words below to form proper and complete sentences. Some sentences can be written more than one way.

1) a / Jordan / teenager / precocious / Romero / very / is
Jordan Romero ______________________________________

2) We / start / better / 'd / training
We ______________________________________

3) Jordan / fat / get / to / never / likely / was
Jordan ______________________________________

4) Jordan's / eager / support / to / his / father / was / his
Jordan's father ______________________________________

Looking Back

1. Read the article again. Circle the correct word choice.

On Christmas Eve 2011, **1) the / a** 15-year-old from California phoned his mother to tell her where **2) he / him** was. He was on the summit of Mount Vinson, overlooking the Ronne Ice Shelf, about 1200 km from the **3) south pole / South Pole**.

At her home in the town of Big Bear, Leigh Anne Drake has received calls, from six similarly elevated locations, in the past five years. **4) At / On** the age of ten, her son had been on the summit of Mount Kilimanjaro. Over the course of 2007, he was on top of Mount Kosciuszko in Australia, Mount Elbrus in Russia and Mount Aconcagua in Argentina. The following year, he ticked off America's Mount McKinley. In 2009, he was on the Carstensz Pyramid in Indonesia.

Last year not long before he graduated from **5) Junior High School / junior high school**, Jordan Romero had called his mother to tell her he had become the youngest climber to reach the top of Mount Everest, at the age of 13.

Now, he has called to say that he was **6) the / a** youngest person to have conquered the seven highest summits on each of the seven continents, as well as climbing Mount Kosciuszko.

"Team Jordan" had set off up their final peak in a snowstorm on Tuesday. On Friday, they ascended **7) the / a** high ridge in bright sunshine and reached the summit shortly before 1 pm, Antarctic time. "I'm the proudest dad in the world right now," said Paul Romero, who has accompanied and chivvied his son to the top of all seven peaks, along with his wife, Karen Lundgren, Jordan Romero's stepmother.

Mr. Romero, an air ambulance paramedic, who may also be due recognition as the world's most competitive father, began preparing his son for these feats after the nine-year-old Jordan pointed to a mural depicting the seven summits, on a wall in his primary school. He said: "Hey dad, I want to climb these mountains." Jordan's father was eager to support his son, and also thought the idea of summiting the peaks sounded like a great adventure.

He was also keen to do it while he was still in his early forties and physically capable of the challenge. He said: “Well then, we’d better start training.” Jordan duly commenced five years of runs, carrying weighted backpacks, and nights spent sleeping in a hypoxic tent, to become accustomed to the thin mountaintop air. “As soon as the sun wakes up, we make waffles, burn down a couple of cups of coffee and just go hard until dark,” Mr. Romero told The Times last year. “We’ve redefined family quality time.”

Mr. Romero has **8) occasional / occasionally** faced criticism for **9) pushing / push** Jordan too hard, too young, particularly after another precocious Californian, Abby Sunderland, 16, had to be rescued while attempting to sail solo around the globe. Mr. Romero defended his vigorous style of parenting by pointing to the unhealthy lifestyles that other parents **10) allow / allowed** their children to lead. Jordan at least, was never likely to get fat.

I’d say ‘I don’t even want to smell a bad attitude today,’ Mr. Romero said, recalling their hike up to Everest Base Camp. “If that didn’t work, it would be, ‘OK, drop and give me 40 pushups.’ It’s amazing what doing 40 push-ups does for your attitude.”

Further up Everest, Jordan, his father and stepmother were engulfed in **11) the / an** avalanche that killed a fellow climber and dragged them down the mountainside towards a crevasse.

“We jokingly told Jordan that he couldn’t tell his mom about it until he was 18,” said Ms. Lundgren.

Yesterday, Ms. Drake would have been pleased to learn that her son was safely back at the base camp beneath Mount Vinson Massif, and preparing to return to California to thank his sponsors, offer his services as a motivational speaker and catch up on his **12) homework / homeworks**.

Moral of the story Know no limits.

2. Answer the following questions related to the story.

1) Do you think Jordan's father pushed him too hard? Why or why not? Should parents push children to do things that are typically reserved for adults?

____

____

____

____

____

2) Do you have a physical or sports related life goal or dream? What is it? How could you begin to train today, in order to achieve it within your lifetime?

____

____

____

____

____

3) Do you think Jordan is brave? Do you think he is foolish? What activities are appropriate for a 15-year old? What were you doing when you were 15?

____

____

____

____

____

Last Chance Glance

Read the job profile below.

Travel Agent

Jordan Romero and his team traveled a lot, in order to summit the tallest peaks on each continent. When people travel, the benefit is from the knowledge and expertise of a travel agent.

Travel agents are mainly responsible for researching and booking travel arrangements for their clients. These travel arrangements may be a honeymoon, family vacation, or business trip. Regardless of the client's reason for traveling, the travel agent should be able to offer advice on the destination and be knowledgeable about making transportation and accommodation recommendations.

These professionals should be able to provide their clients with a wealth of information regarding their destination. Data such as expected weather conditions, travel advisories, and documentation requirements should be part of the information provided to customers. Travel agents must keep abreast of developments in foreign countries that may influence travel arrangements or may make a particular destination unsafe for travel.

The more education a travel agent obtains, the greater their opportunities will be for advancement and better salary. It is also useful for travel agents to receive some education in other areas like language, history, geography, and business. History and geography knowledge will help the agent research destinations and make better-informed recommendations.

The American Society of Travel Agents is the largest professional travel agent organization in the world. Their main role is to advocate for travel professionals and the travel industry. The association's mission is to facilitate the sale of travel products, and membership in this organization signals the experience and professionalism of the travel agent.

Unit 8

Jamie Oliver: A Food Revolution

Vocabulary Preview

Create a story using the following words.

pub	venture	petition
nutritionist	dietician	catering
processed	nutritious	self-employed

A First Look

1. Read the article below about a famous, inspiring or noteworthy person.

Jamie Oliver: A Food Revolution

Born on 27 May 1975, Jamie Oliver took an early interest in food. He grew up in Essex, where his parents Trevor and Sally still run their own highly respected pub / restaurant the Cricketers, and was frequently found helping out in the kitchens. His fascination for food continued to grow. At 16, Jamie left school and completed his training at Westminster Catering College. After spending some time working in France, followed by a stint in London, Jamie joined the acclaimed River Café, where he worked for three and a half years.

In 2004, motivated by the poor state of school food in the UK, Jamie embarked on one of his most ambitious ventures. He went back to school with the aim of educating and motivating the children and the school cooks to enjoy cooking and eating healthy, nutritious lunches, rather than the processed foods that they were used to. Jamie launched a national campaign called Feed Me Better, and launched an online petition for better school meals. As a result of the 271,677 signatures on the petition, the government pledged an extra £280 million to improve the standard of school meals, to provide training for school cooks and purchase equipment for schools. Jamie was still worried though, and continued to fight for the health of school children, but this time he went to the United States.

"Jamie Oliver's Food Revolution" premiered in the US in March 2010. In order to promote his campaign to improve school lunches in the United States, Jamie appeared on Oprah to launch the campaign and also carried out high profile interviews on Letterman, Leno and Nightline, as well as press interviews in the New York Times and TIME magazine. Although Jamie films his work for a television show, the results are real. He is a chef and entrepreneur that is changing the way schools feed children. Jamie became the recipient of the prestigious TED award for 2010.

Jamie is well known for his outspoken views on banning chocolate and strawberry flavored milks from school cafeterias. He says they are loaded with sugar, and just one extra serving a day can increase a child's risk of developing obesity by 60%. He also believes that school lunches should include two portions of fruit and three vegetables each day. He has faced his critics, though, many of who say that the cost of healthy lunches is too high. Jamie, on the other hand, believes there is no substitute for fresh, wholesome food and continues to battle for the health of America's children.

Moral of the story A healthy body supports a healthy mind.

2. Answer each question below. Circle the correct answer.

1) Where is Jamie Oliver from?

A. The UK

B. London

C. The US

D. Australia

2) How did Jamie become interested in food?

A. He always wanted to become a chef.

B. His parents sent him to cooking school.

C. His parents owned a restaurant.

D. He left school and needed a job.

3) Why did Jamie start a 'food revolution'?

A. He was concerned about the health of school children.

B. He thought school lunches were balanced.

C. He wanted to create a successful television show.

D. He wanted to become famous.

4) What is Jamie well known for?

A. He is known for his accent.

B. He is known for his popular television shows.

C. He is known for his campaign against strawberry and chocolate flavored milks.

D. He is known for his anti-milk campaign.

5) What is the goal of the 'food revolution'?

A. Improve the quality of lunches and therefore the health of children.

B. Teach the cooks and children about the importance of fresh, wholesome food.

C. Ban sugary snacks from school cafeterias.

D. All of the above are true.

A Closer Look

1. Use the following phrases in complete sentences.

1) with the aim of

____

2) rather than

____

3) were used to

____

4) continued to

____

5) is well known for

____

2. Rewrite the words below to form proper and complete sentences. Some sentences can be written more than one way.

1) Jamie / school / healthy / lunch / of / advocate / an / is

Jamie ____

2) Jamie / campaign / a / national / launched

Jamie ____

3) He / fight / continued / for / to / school / children / the / of / health

He ____

4) be / wants / school / to / and / happy / Jamie / healthy / children

Jamie ____

Looking Back

1. Read the article again. Circle the correct word choice.

Born **1) in / on** 27 May 1975, Jamie Oliver took an early **2) interest / interested** in food. He grew up in Essex, where his parents Trevor and Sally still run their own highly respected pub / restaurant The Cricketers, and was frequently found helping out in the kitchens. His **3) fascinating / fascination** for food continued to grow. At 16, Jamie **4) left / leave** school and completed his training at Westminster Catering College. After spending some time working **5) in / at** France, followed by a stint in London, Jamie joined **6) an / the** acclaimed River Café, where he worked for three and a half years.

In 2004, **7) motivated / motivating** by the poor state of school food in the UK, Jamie embarked on one of his most ambitious ventures. He went back to school with the aim of educating and motivating the children and the school cooks to enjoy cooking and eating healthy, nutritious lunches, rather than the processed foods that they were used to. Jamie launched a national campaign called Feed Me Better, and launched an **8) Online / online** petition for better school meals. As a result of the 271,677 signatures on the petition, the government pledged an extra £280 million to improve the standard of school meals, to provide training for school cooks and purchase equipment for schools. Jamie was still worried though, and continued to fight for the heath of school children, but this time he went to **9) The / the** United States.

"Jamie Oliver's Food Revolution" premiered in the US in March 2010. In order to promote his campaign to improve school lunches in the United States, Jamie appeared on Oprah to launch the campaign and also carried out high profile interviews on Letterman, Leno and Nightline, as well as press interviews in The New York Times and TIME magazine. Although Jamie films his work for a television show, the results are real. He is a chef and entrepreneur **10) that, / that** is changing the way schools feed children. Jamie became the recipient of **11) a /**

the prestigious TED award for 2010.

Jamie is well known for his outspoken views on banning chocolate and strawberry flavored milks from school cafeterias. He says they are loaded with sugar, and just one extra serving a day can increase a child's risk of developing obesity by 60%. He also believes that school lunches should include two portions of fruit and three vegetables each day. He has faced his critics, though, many of who say that the cost of healthy lunches is too high. Jamie, on the other hand, believes there is no substitute for fresh, wholesome food and continues to **12) battling / battle** for the heath of America's children.

Moral of the story A healthy body supports a healthy mind.

2. Answer the following questions related to the story.

1) Does your country provide students with fresh and wholesome school lunches? Why or why not?

____

____

____

____

____

2) What can be done in your own community to safeguard against obesity and diabetes?

____

____

____

____

____

3) How important do you think nutrition is? Is it more important than exercise? Is it more important that getting good grades?

____

____

____

____

____

Last Chance Glance

Read the job profile below.

Nutritionist / Dietician

Dieticians and nutritionists plan food and nutrition programs, and supervise the preparation and serving of meals. They help prevent and treat illnesses by promoting healthy eating habits and suggesting diet modifications. Dietitians run food service systems for institutions such as hospitals and schools, promote sound eating habits through education, and conduct research. Major areas of practice include clinical, community, management, and consultant dietetics.

Dietitians and nutritionists need at least a bachelor's degree in dietetics, foods and nutrition, food service systems management, or food science. College students in these majors take courses in foods, nutrition, institution management, chemistry, biochemistry, biology, microbiology, and physiology. Other suggested courses include business, mathematics, statistics, computer science, psychology, sociology, and economics.

Experienced dietitians may advance to assistant, associate, or director of a dietetic department, or become self-employed. Some dietitians specialize in areas such as pediatric dietetics. Others may leave the occupation to become sales representatives for equipment, pharmaceutical, or food manufacturers.

Employment of dietitians is expected to grow as fast as the average for all occupations through 2018. A growing and aging population will increase the demand for meals and nutritional counseling in nursing homes, schools, prisons, community health programs, and home health care agencies.

Unit 9

Nando Parrado: Miracle in the Andes

Vocabulary Preview

Create a story using the following words.

survivor	wreck	teammates
skull	obituary	mortician
frail	raw	flesh

A First Look

1. Read the article below about a famous, inspiring or noteworthy person.

Nando Parrado: Miracle in the Andes

Nando Parrado was born in Montevideo, Uruguay, to a middle-class family. From early age, he demonstrated special skills for sports and excelled in rugby. He eventually became captain of his college team.

In November 1972, he flew to Chile with his teammates for an international match. Unfortunately, the flight never arrived; it tragically crashed at 18,000 feet in the Andes Mountains. Three days later, Nando Parrado woke from a coma, a ball of snow held up to his mouth by a fellow survivor. His skull was fractured, but he was alive. His little sister, who had been on the flight, was barely alive; his mother was dead.

Forty-five passengers and crew had been aboard the aircraft. Of these, 32 survived the impact, including one of the pilots. He was trapped and so badly injured that he begged for the revolver he kept in his flight bag. In the first days, Parrado nursed his sister and took stock of the situation. The odds of survival were almost zero. They were stuck at 12,000 feet, dressed in short-sleeved summer shirts, many of them with appalling wounds.

Marcelo Perez, the captain of the team, had taken charge in the most heroic way. He hunted the baggage for food, had the dead pulled out and buried, and organized the building of a snow wall to plug the end of the fuselage. Without this insulation, no one would have lived through the first night. But most of all, he coaxed the living to keep faith.

With no proper supplies, the wounded began to die. Parrado's sister died in his arms, while he himself had to wait for nature to repair "the shattered fragments" of his skull. The living had nothing to drink, except a few daily drops of snow, melted by the sun. And then there was the matter of food; he and his companions faced the grim reality of survival. If they did not eat the raw flesh of their dead comrades, they would die. "I knew those bodies represented our only chance of survival," he later wrote. From that moment on, the survivors ate the flesh of their friends, with the identity of the dead always kept a secret.

Soon after, a frail transistor radio broadcasted the dreadful truth; the search to save them had been called off. Morale plummeted. The only hope of survival was to send a team for help. Parrado and three others volunteered to go − to scale the sky-scraping peaks that stood between them and civilization. But before they could leave, an avalanche in the night killed eight more members, including their gallant captain, Perez, and temporarily trapped the rest of them in the wreck.

Finally, packing the warmest clothes and a supply of human meat as food, Parrado and his expedition set off over the mountains in search of salvation. Eventually, after 10 days of indescribable hardship and a total of more than 70 days in the Andes, he and one of his companions spotted a peasant on the far bank of a roaring river. Parrado scribbled a note, tied it to a stone and threw it across. It began "I come from a plane that fell into the mountains…."

Moral of the story When the going gets tough, the tough get going.

2. Answer each question below. Circle the correct answer.

1) How long was Nando Parrado in the Andes?
   A. More than 50 days
   B. More than 70 days
   C. 3 months
   D. 4 months

2) What event did NOT occur in the mountains?
   A. He ate human flesh.
   B. He buried his sister.
   C. He learned to play rugby.
   D. He wore summer clothes.

3) Which of Nando's family members were also passengers?
   A. His younger brother and mother
   B. His younger sister and mother
   C. His older sister and mother
   D. His father and mother

4) How did Nando communicate with the farmer he saw after walking for 10 days?
   A. He yelled across a roaring river.
   B. He and his friend yelled together.
   C. He tied a note to a rock and threw it across the river.
   D. He swam across the river.

5) Why was Nando on the airplane?
   A. He was going to Uruguay to play rugby.
   B. He was going on vacation with his rugby team.
   C. He was going on vacation with his mother and sister.
   D. He was going to Chile to play rugby.

A Closer Look

1. Use the following phrases in complete sentences.

1) flew to

____

2) take charge in

____

3) from an early age

____

4) from that moment on

____

5) in search of

____

2. Rewrite the words below to form proper and complete sentences. Some sentences can be written more than one way.

1) saved / survivors / the / of / the / Nando / lives

Nando ____

2) Andes / occurred / A / the / miracle / Mountains / in

A miracle ____________________________________

3) Parrado / sister / nursed / his

Parrado ______________________________________

4) Crew / the / been / aircraft / aboard / had

Crew ____

Looking Back

1. Read the article again. Circle the correct word choice.

Nando Parrado was born in Montevideo, Uruguay, to a middle-class family. From early age, he **1) demonstrating / demonstrated** special **2) skills / skill** for sports and **3) excelling / excelled** in rugby. He eventually **4) became / become** captain of his college team.

In November 1972, he **5) flew / flied** to Chile with his teammates for **6) an / a** international match. Unfortunately, the flight never arrived; it tragically crashed at 18,000 feet in the Andes Mountains. Three days later, Nando Parrado woke from a coma, a ball of snow held up to his mouth **7) for / by** a fellow survivor. His skull was fractured, but he was alive. His little sister, who **8) had / has** been on the flight, was barely alive; his mother was **9) died / dead.**

Forty-five passengers and crew had been aboard the aircraft. **10) For / Of** these, 32 survived the impact, including one of the pilots. He was trapped and so badly injured that he **11) bagged / begged** for the revolver he kept in his flight bag. In the first days, Parrado nursed his sister and took stock of the situation. The odds of survival were almost zero. They were stuck at 12,000 feet, dressed in short-sleeved summer shirts, many of them with appalling wounds.

Marcelo Perez, the captain of the team, had taken charge in the most heroic way. He hunted **12) a / the** baggage for food, had the dead pulled out and buried, and organized the building of a snow wall to plug the end of the fuselage. Without this insulation, no one would have lived through the first night. But most of **13) them / all**, he coaxed the living to keep faith.

With **14) no / none** proper supplies, the wounded began to die. Parrado's sister died in his arms, while he himself had to wait for nature to repair "the shattered fragments" of his skull. The living had nothing to drink, except a few daily drops of snow, melted by the sun. And then there was the matter of food; he and his companions faced the grim reality of survival. If they did not eat the raw flesh of their dead comrades, they would die. "I knew those bodies represented our only chance of survival," he later wrote. From that moment on, the survivors ate the flesh of their friends, with the identity of the dead always **15) keep / kept** a secret.

Soon after, a frail transistor radio broadcasted the dreadful truth; the search to save them had been called off. Morale plummeted. The only **16) hopes / hope** of survival was to send a team for help. Parrado and three others volunteered to go - to scale the sky-scraping **17) peaks / peeks** that stood between them and civilization. But before they could leave, an avalanche in the night killed eight more members, including their **18) giant / gallant** captain, Perez, and temporarily trapped the rest of them in the wreck.

Finally, packing the warmest clothes and a supply of human meat as food, Parrado and his expedition set off over the mountains in search of salvation. Eventually, after 10 days of indescribable hardship and a total of more than 70 days in the Andes, he and one of his companions spotted a **19) pheasant / peasant** on the far bank of a roaring river. Parrado scribbled a note, tied it to a stone and **20) through / threw** it across. It began "I come from a plane that fell into the mountains…."

Moral of the story When the going gets tough, the tough get going.

2. Answer the following questions related to the story.

1) Why is having hope and faith important when someone faces a difficult situation?

____

____

____

____

____

2) What is the most difficult situation you have faced? How did you overcome your difficulty? How did you feel when it was over?

____

____

____

____

____

3) Is eating the flesh of humans morally or ethically wrong? What about in a survival situation? What would you do if you were faced with the decision to eat human flesh, or die?

____

____

____

____

____

Last Chance Glance

Read the job profile below.

Funeral Director

Funeral directors arrange funeral services and burials. They work in funeral homes, where bodies are kept until cremation or burial. Funeral directors are sometimes called morticians or undertakers.

When funeral directors are notified of a death, they arrange for the body to be moved to the funeral home. They get the information needed for the death certificate and for the newspaper death notice, or obituary. They meet with the family of the deceased to discuss the details of the funeral service, including the selection of a casket, if the body is to be embalmed. Funeral directors help the family to set the time and location for burial, arrange for a member of the clergy to conduct any religious services, and choose pallbearers. Once these plans have been made, they contact cemetery officials, the clergy, and the newspapers.

Funeral directors need to know about the funeral customs of various religious, ethnic, and fraternal groups. They must also be familiar with the laws dealing with the handling of bodies. Since many funeral directors are also licensed embalmers, they may prepare the body for burial. They arrange the casket in a parlor and take care of lighting and flower arrangements. They stay in the parlor to greet and comfort the family and friends of the deceased and to make sure that the services run as planned. They also arrange transportation to the cemetery or crematorium for the family and pallbearers. Funeral directors lead the funeral procession to the church or cemetery, where they may help direct the service. If burial is to be in another area, they oversee the preparation and shipment of the body.

Funeral directors may also help the family of the deceased with insurance claims. They may serve the family for several months until they have taken care of these and other details.

Unit 10

Narayanan Krishnan: A Chef and Hero

Vocabulary Preview

Create a story using the following words.

chef	compassion	sponsor
destitute	undecaying	imperishable
nook	crannies	subsidize

A First Look

1. Read the article below about a famous, inspiring or noteworthy person.

Narayanan Krishnan: A Chef and Hero

Narayanan Krishnan was a bright, young, award-winning chef with a five-star hotel group, short-listed for an elite job in Switzerland. But a quick visit home to India, before heading to Europe, changed everything.

Krishnan was visiting a temple in the south Indian city of Madurai in 2002, when he saw the man under a bridge. While he was raised in India, a country stricken with poverty and hunger, Krishnan was not prepared for what he was about to see. He saw an elderly man eat his own human waste, out of sheer desperation and hunger. He began to feed that man, and at that moment, Krishnan believes, his destiny was born. Haunted by the image, Krishnan quit his job within the week and returned home for good, convinced of his new destiny.

Krishnan founded his nonprofit Akshaya Trust in 2003. Now 29, he has served more than 1.2 million meals – breakfast, lunch and dinner – to India's homeless and destitute, mostly elderly people abandoned by their families and often abused.

Krishnan said the name Akshaya is Sanskrit for "undecaying" or "imperishable," and was chosen "to signify that human compassion should never decay or perish ... The spirit of helping others must prevail for ever." Also, in Hindu mythology, Goddess Annapoorani's "Akshaya bowl" fed the hungry endlessly, never depleting its resources.

Krishnan sites the panic and suffering of human hunger as his driving force. His day begins at 4 a.m. He and his team cover nearly 125 miles in a donated van, routinely working in temperatures topping 100 degrees Fahrenheit. He seeks out the homeless under bridges and in the nooks and crannies between the city's temples. The hot meals he delivers are simple, tasty vegetarian fare he personally prepares, packs and often hand-feeds to nearly 400 clients each day. Krishnan carries a comb, scissors and razor and is trained in eight haircut styles that, along with a fresh shave, provide extra dignity to those he serves.

He says many of the homeless seldom know their names or origins, and none has the capacity to beg, ask for help or offer thanks. They may be paranoid and hostile because of their conditions, but Krishnan says this only steadies his resolve to offer help.

The group's operations cost about $327 a day, but sponsored donations only cover 22 days a month. Krishnan subsidizes the shortfall with $88 he receives in monthly rent from a home his grandfather gave him.

For lack of funding, the organization has been forced to halt construction on Akshaya Home, Krishnan's vision of a dormitory where he can provide shelter for the people he helps. Despite the demands and few comforts his lifestyle affords, Krishnan says he's enjoying his life.

"Now I am feeling so comfortable and so happy," he says. "I have a passion, I enjoy my work. I want to live with my people."

Moral of the story It's better to give than to receive.

2. Answer each question below. Circle the correct answer.

1) How old is Krishnan now?
   A. His age is not given in the story.
   B. 22 years old
   C. 29 years old
   D. 42 years old

2) Where was Krishnan going to work?
   A. He was going to work in India.
   B. He was going to work in Switzerland.
   C. He was going to work in New York.
   D. He was going to work in Japan.

3) Why did Krishnan start feeding the hungry?
   A. He is a chef and cooks well.
   B. His mother wanted him to.
   C. He saw humans go to waste.
   D. He saw a man eat human waste.

4) What is the cost of his program?
   A. $327 a day
   B. $88 a day
   C. $22 a day
   D. $400 a day

5) Who prepares the food he serves?
   A. Krishnan prepares it.
   B. Krishnan's mother prepares it.
   C. Krishnan's team prepares it.
   D. Krishnan and his team prepare it.

A Closer Look

1. Use the following phrases in complete sentences.

1) for lack of

____

2) was raised

____

3) for good

____

4) convinced of

____

5) for ever

____

2. Rewrite the words below to form proper and complete sentences. Some sentences can be written more than one way.

1) His / at / day / begins / 4 a.m.
His day ____

2) everyday / people / feeds / He / hungry
He ____

3) He / home / good / for / returned
He ____

4) Many / homeless / the / know / their / seldom / names / of
Many of the homeless ________________________________

Looking Back

1. Read the article again. Circle the correct word choice.

Narayanan Krishnan was a bright, young, **1) award winning / award-winning** chef with a five-star hotel group, **2) short-listed / short listed** for an elite job in Switzerland. But a quick visit home to India, before heading to Europe, changed **3) every thing / everything**.

Krishnan was visiting a temple in the **4) South / south** Indian city of Madurai in 2002, when he saw the man under a bridge. While he was raised in India, a country stricken with poverty and hunger, Krishnan was not **5) prepare / prepared** for what he was about to see. He saw an elderly man eat his own human waste, out of sheer desperation and hunger. He began to feed that man, and at that moment, Krishnan believes, his destiny was born. Haunted by the image, Krishnan quit his job **6) with in / within** the week and returned home for good, **7) convincing / convinced** of his new destiny.

Krishnan **8) founded / found** his nonprofit Akshaya Trust in 2003. Now 29, he has served more than 1.2 million meals – breakfast, lunch and dinner – to India's homeless and destitute, mostly elderly people abandoned by their families and often abused.

Krishnan said the name Akshaya is Sanskrit for "undecaying" or "imperishable," and was chosen "to signify [that] human compassion should never decay or perish. ... The spirit of helping others must prevail for ever." Also, in Hindu mythology, Goddess Annapoorani's "Akshaya bowl" fed the **9) hunger / hungry** endlessly, never depleting its resources.

Krishnan sites the **10) panic / panicking** and suffering of human hunger as his driving force. His day begins at 4 a.m. He and his team cover nearly 125 miles in a donated van, routinely working in temperatures topping 100 degrees Fahrenheit.

He seeks out the homeless under bridges and in the nooks and crannies between the city's temples. The hot meals he delivers are simple, tasty vegetarian fare he personally prepares, packs and often hand-feeds to nearly 400 clients each day. Krishnan carries a comb, scissors and razor and is trained in eight haircut styles that, along with a fresh shave, provide extra dignity to those he serves.

He says many of the homeless seldom know their names or origins, and none has the capacity to beg, ask for help or offer thanks. They may be paranoid and hostile because of their conditions, but Krishnan says this only **11) steadys / steadies** his resolve to offer help.

The group's operations cost about $327 a day, but sponsored donations only cover 22 days a month. Krishnan subsidizes the shortfall with $88 he **12) recieves / receives** in monthly rent from a home his grandfather gave him.

For lack of funding, the organization has been forced to halt construction on Akshaya Home, Krishnan's vision of a dormitory where he can provide shelter for the people he helps. Despite the demands and few comforts his lifestyle affords, Krishnan says he's enjoying his life.

"Now I am feeling so comfortable and so happy," he says. "I have a passion, I enjoy my work. I want to live with my people."

Moral of the story It's better to give than to receive.

2. Answer the following questions related to the story.

1) Was it foolish of Krishnan to give up his dream of being a chef to help the hungry? Why or why not?

2) How can you help the less fortunate in your own country? What are some of the social or economic issues you would like to address?

3) Can one person really make a difference with issues like hunger or homelessness? Is Krishnan's work about doing something for himself, or doing something for others?

Last Chance Glance

Read the job profile below.

Chef

In French, the word *chef* means "chief." A head chef, also sometimes referred to as "chef de cuisine" or "executive chef," is in charge of the whole kitchen. Every part of a foodservice operation, including menu planning, purchasing, hiring and staffing, is part of a head chef's job description. That means he or she also has the overall responsibility for all the food that comes out of the kitchen. With that said, the head chef doesn't actually cook. They have many chefs under them who cook the menu they approve.

Sous Chef / Second Chef

The sous chef (pronounced "SOO chef," from the French word for *under*) is in charge of all the cooking. In some kitchens, the sous chef's job is to directly supervise the entire kitchen staff, including the line cooks, prep cooks and dishwashers. While his or her job is still mainly supervisory, the sous chef may also do some actual cooking, for instance, stepping in to replace one of the line cooks if necessary. A sous chef's job description also frequently includes expediting, or relaying orders to the line cooks and ensuring that the team works together to get all the orders right and get them out promptly.

Chef de Partie / Station Chef

A chef de partie ("chef duh-par-TEE") is the person whose job it is to work a station on the hot cooking line. Usually called *line cooks,* they're the ones doing the real cooking. Though every kitchen is organized differently, most will have, at a minimum, the following line cooks: sauté cook, roast cook and vegetable cook.

Unit 11

Matt Long: A Second Chance

Vocabulary Preview

Create a story using the following words.

firefighter	triathlete	pavement
recovery	protection	flank
lane	stride	pelvis

A First Look

1. Read the article below about a famous, inspiring or noteworthy person.

Matt Long: A Second Chance

Huffing and hobbling along the running path in Central Park, Matthew Long stands out against the smooth-striding runners swarming the park to prepare for the New York City Marathon.

Mr. Long, a New York City firefighter and a former triathlete and competitive marathoner, once had a smooth, swift stride himself, but he was critically injured when a chartered bus hit him as he was biking to work during the transit workers' strike in December 2005.

The bus pinned him and his bicycle to the pavement at a Midtown intersection. He underwent three days of emergency operations, and received more than 60 pints of blood.

Much credit is given to the paramedics who arrived first at the scene of Matt's accident; their quick response likely saved his life. He was taken to New York Presbyterian Hospital, where doctors spent several days just trying to keep him alive, then began to treat extensive damage to his right shoulder, pelvis, both legs and a foot, and repair severe injuries to his torso and gastrointestinal system. He needed skin grafts and muscle grafts, and parts of his body had to be rebuilt.

Doctors said Mr. Long's fine physical condition helped him survive. He had been working as a fitness instructor at the Fire Academy on Randalls Island and had just run the New York City Marathon in 3 hours 13 minutes 59 seconds, an average of 7 minutes 20 seconds per mile. He was training for the Boston Marathon.

After the accident, he had to learn to walk again, but he told his physical therapists in 2008 that he would take his salvaged body, rebuilt with pins and screws and rods, and compete in the New York City Marathon on Nov. 2.

In May of 2008, he did a mile – for the first time since the accident – in 24 minutes, the pace of a brisk walk. Then he was down to 14 minutes. Although it seemed impossible, Matt Long was dedicated to recovery.

"I wanted to do it on the grandest of running stages," said Mr. Long, who wore his orthopedic sneakers and F.D.N.Y. T-shirt and made the best of his running stride, with its awkward hitch. Two friends, for balance, protection and support, flanked him.

Mr. Long's motivation is the sum of many things: 40 operations; 5 months in the hospital; the fear that he would never walk again; and a sense of valor tested at the World Trade Center on 9/11, where he helped rescue trapped comrades.

Before the accident, Mr. Long had finished 30 triathlons of various lengths, including the 2005 Ironman in Lake Placid, N.Y., in which he ran the marathon part in 3 hours 44 minutes, after swimming 2.4 miles and biking 112 miles.

The bus hit him when it turned right from the center lane of Third Avenue onto 52nd Street. The driver, who received a ticket for the turn, said he never saw Mr. Long, who was traveling uptown on Third Avenue.

Chances are slim that Mr. Long will ever fight fires again, but he has returned to work at the academy, giving motivational talks to new firefighters.

Since his first marathon, Matt has gone on to train hard and complete more full marathons, and successfully finished a triathlon. He recently participated in the World Police and Firefighter Games.

Moral of the story Believing in yourself is the first step to success.

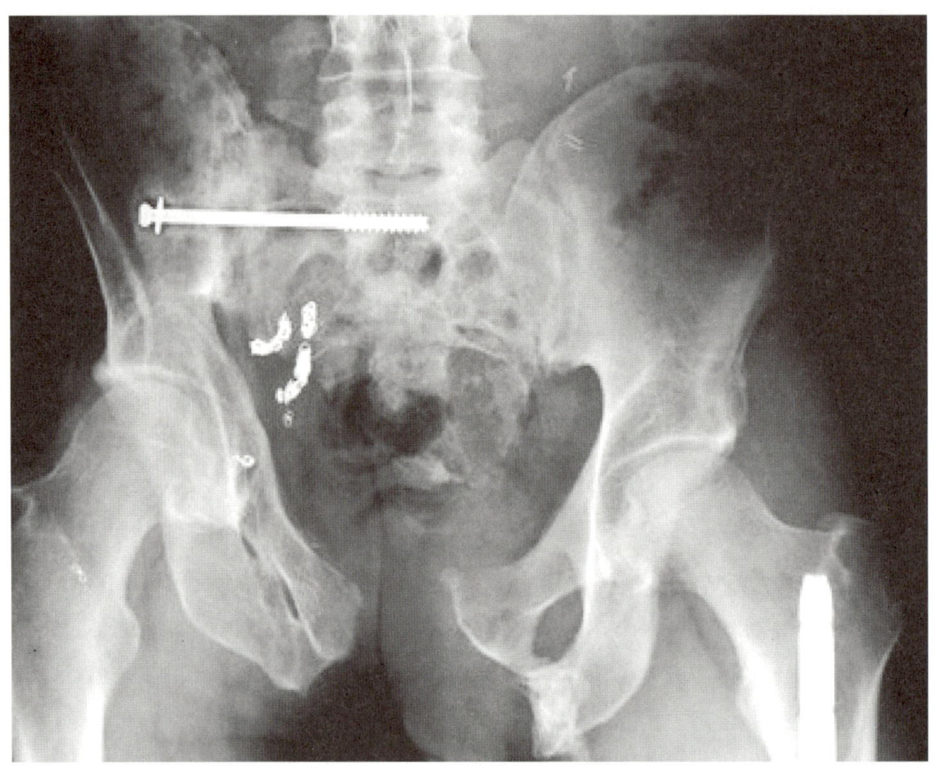

NYC

2. Answer each question below. Circle the correct answer.

1) What was Matt's job before his accident?
   A. He was a professional athlete.
   B. He was a firefighter and trainer at the fire academy.
   C. He was a bus driver.
   D. He was a bicycle deliveryman.

2) Where did his motivation come from?
   A. A sense of valor from being in the 9/11 World Trade Center attacks in New York
   B. A sense of valor from being a firefighter
   C. A sense of valor from being an athlete
   D. Having good doctors

3) What happened to Matt?
   A. He was hit by a bus on his way to school.
   B. He was driving a bus and hit someone.
   C. He was hit by a bus on his way to work.
   D. None of the above.

4) What was Matt's accomplishment in 2005?
   A. He became a marathoner.
   B. He became a father.
   C. He became an Ironman.
   D. He was hit by a bus.

5) What does Matt do for a living now?
   A. He is still a firefighter.
   B. He is a professional athlete.
   C. He does not work.
   D. He works for the fire department, but is not a firefighter.

A Closer Look

1. Use the following phrases in complete sentences.

1) after the accident

____

2) at the scene of

____

3) for the first time since

____

4) give credit to

____

5) was taken to

____

2. Rewrite the words below to form proper and complete sentences. Some sentences can be written more than one way.

1) He / again / walk / to / learn / had / to
He ____

2) Long / recovery / to / dedicated / was
Long ____

3) Mr. Long / again / fires / fight / will / not
Mr. Long ____

4) Matt / firefighter / New York / was / a / for / City
Matt ____

Looking Back

1. Read the article again. Circle the correct word choice.

Huffing and hobbling along the running path in Central Park, Matthew Long stands out against the smooth-striding runners swarming the park to prepare for the New York City Marathon.

Mr. Long, a New York City firefighter and a former triathlete and competitive marathoner, once had a smooth, swift stride himself, but he was critically **1) injured / injuring** when a chartered bus hit him as he was **2) biked / biking** to work during the transit workers' strike in December 2005.

The bus pinned him and his bicycle to the pavement at a Midtown intersection. He **3) undergo / underwent** three days of emergency operations, and received more than 60 pints of blood.

Much **4) care / credit** is given to the paramedics who arrived first at the scene of Matt's accident; their quick response likely saved his life. He was **5) taking / taken** to New York Presbyterian Hospital, where doctors spent several days just trying to keep him alive, then began to treat extensive damage to his right shoulder, pelvis, both legs and a foot, and repair severe injuries to his torso and gastrointestinal system. He needed skin grafts and muscle grafts, and parts of his body had to be **6) rebuilding / rebuilt**.

Doctors said Mr. Long's fine physical condition helped him survive. He had been working as a fitness instructor at the Fire Academy on Randalls Island and had just run the New York City Marathon in 3 hours 13 minutes 59 seconds, an average of 7 minutes 20 seconds per mile. He was training for the Boston Marathon.

After the accident, he had to learn to walk again, but he told his physical therapists in 2008 that he would take his salvaged body, rebuilt with pins and screws and rods, and compete in the New York City Marathon on Nov. 2.

In May of 2008, he did a mile — for the first time since the accident — in 24 minutes, the pace of a brisk walk. Then he was down to 14 minutes. Although it seemed impossible, Matt Long was dedicated to recovery.

"I wanted to do it on the grandest of running stages," said Mr. Long, who wore his orthopedic **7) sneaker / sneakers** and F.D.N.Y. T-shirt and made the best of his running stride, with its awkward hitch. Two friends, for balance, protection and support, flanked him.

Mr. Long's motivation is the sum of many things: 40 operations; 5 months in the hospital; the fear that he would never walk again; and a sense of valor tested at the World Trade Center on 9/11, where he helped rescue trapped comrades.

Before the accident, Mr. Long had finished 30 triathlons of various lengths, including the 2005 Ironman in Lake Placid, N.Y., in which he ran the marathon part in 3 hours 44 minutes, after swimming 2.4 miles and biking 112 miles.

The bus hit him when it turned right from the center **8) line / lane** of Third Avenue onto 52nd Street. The driver, who received a ticket for the turn, said he never saw Mr. Long, who was traveling uptown on Third Avenue.

Chances are slim that Mr. Long will ever **9) do / fight** fires again, but he has returned to work at the academy, giving motivational talks to new firefighters.

Since his first marathon, Matt has gone on to train hard and complete more full marathons, and successfully finished a triathlon. He recently participated **10) in / for** the World Police and Firefighter Games.

Moral of the story Believing in yourself is the first step to success.

2. Answer the following questions related to the story.

1) What do you think was the most important factor in Matt's recovery?

____

____

____

____

____

2) Why was Matt able to overcome so many difficulties and become an athlete again?

____

____

____

____

____

3) Who should be held responsible, if anyone, for Matt's accident? Matt? The bus driver? The union? The city of New York? Why?

____

____

____

____

____

Last Chance Glance

Read the job profile below.

Paramedics

Working as a paramedic can be a rewarding career. Paramedics should be well trained, and respond quickly in high-pace and stressful situations. The hours of work are variable due to the need to provide emergency services on a 24-hour basis. Paramedics work both indoors and outdoors under a variety of weather conditions. The work can be physically and emotionally demanding when transporting patients, responding to emergencies or dealing with critically ill or injured individuals. Some risks are involved, such as exposure to diseases.

Paramedics perform some or all of the following duties:

1. Assess extent of injuries or illness of trauma victims, patients with respiratory disease and stress, overdose and poisoning victims, industrial accident victims and other ill or injured individuals to determine emergency medical treatment.
2. Liaise with ambulance dispatch centers, base hospital staff, police, fire, and family members to ensure relevant information is collected and proper treatment is administered.
3. Administer pre-hospital emergency care, such as cardiopulmonary resuscitation (CPR), oxygen, bandaging and splinting to patients.
4. Establish and maintain intravenous treatment (IV), apply adjunctive equipment for ventilation and circulation complications, administer medications and provide other emergency treatment to patients.
5. Transport patients by air, land or water to hospital or other medical facility for further medical care.
6. Document and record nature of injuries and treatment provided.
7. Maintain ambulances and emergency care equipment and supplies.

Unit 12

Ted Williams: The Man with the Golden Voice

Vocabulary Preview

Create a story using the following words.

addiction	rehabilitation	therapy
aftercare	compassionate	disheveled
upload	pledge	admit

A First Look

1. Read the article below about a famous, inspiring or noteworthy person.

Ted Williams: The Man with the Golden Voice

Ted Williams, born on September 22, 1957, has a God-given talent of voice; at least that's what the cardboard sign said, as he waited near the road, next to a lane of traffic. Ted was asking for donations. He was homeless, and had been struggling with drug and alcohol addiction for years.

On January 3, 2011, Doral Chenweth, a videographer for the *Columbus Dispatch*, recorded an interview with Ted. During the interview, Ted improvised a professional quality radio advertisement. He had a golden voice; the most soothing and unique baritone voice rolled out of the mouth of a homeless man. Doral knew Ted was special.

During the interview, Ted spoke more about his education and what happened to him, and what events lead up to him becoming homeless. In the video, Ted appeared disheveled, and dirty, but had the voice of an angel.

Doral posted the interview on the Internet, and later it was uploaded to the popular video-sharing site YouTube. By January 5th, Ted was receiving attention from national news and media outlets, pledging interviews, job offers, money and clothes. By the end of the week, Ted was offered jobs from MSNBC, the Cleveland Cavaliers, Kraft Foods, and Quicken Loans Arena.

Although Ted claims to have been sober since mid-2008, he began to drink again after the media attention began. During the month of January 2011, Ted met with popular TV psychologist Phil McGraw, and admitted to drinking alcohol heavily again. He agreed to go to a male-only drug rehab facility in Texas arranged by Dr. Phil. Ted left the facility after only 12 days. He stated that he desired more anonymity, and that the whole experience felt "scripted." After that, Ted signed reality television deals and book contracts, but in the spring of 2011, Ted yet again returned to an alcohol rehabilitation center. He put his career on hold until he could manage his addiction.

As it stands, Ted Williams is out of rehab, having finished his program successfully. He has signed another contract to be the official voice of New England Cable News, and works out of his in-home studio in Dublin, Ohio.

Although Ted will always have to manage his addictions with drugs and alcohol, like other recovering addicts, he has been given a second chance to show the world his God-given talent of voice.

Moral of the story Even if you're down, you're still not out.

Ted, as he was first seen, by millions of viewers on YouTube.

Ted, months after being re-discovered.

A younger Ted Williams.

2. Answer each question below. Circle the correct answer.

1) What talent does Ted Williams have?
   A. He has a beautiful smile.
   B. He has a beautiful voice.
   C. He has beautiful eyes.
   D. He has a golden opportunity.

2) When did the videographer record Ted?
   A. January 3, 2011
   B. January 5, 2011
   C. Mid-2008
   D. January 2, 2010

3) Who is Phil McGraw?
   A. A popular TV medical doctor
   B. A popular TV dentist
   C. A popular TV psychiatrist
   D. None of the above

4) Where does Ted currently work?
   A. He works at MSNBC.
   B. He works for a reality TV show.
   C. He is currently in a rehabilitation program and not working.
   D. He works out of his home.

5) Why was Ted in a rehabilitation program?
   A. He was there because he was homeless.
   B. He was there because he was drinking and driving.
   C. He was there because he was drinking heavily.
   D. He was there because Dr. Phil asked him to go.

A Closer Look

1. Use the following phrases in complete sentences.

1) was asking for

____

2) at least

____

3) happened to

____

4) put on hold

____

5) has been struggling with

____

2. Rewrite the words below to form proper and complete sentences. Some sentences can be written more than one way.

1) man / Williams / voice / is / a / a / golden / Ted / with
Ted ______________________________________

2) Ted / who / recovering / homeless / alcoholic / to / is / use / be / a
Ted ______________________________________

3) beautiful / a / use / was / his / to / He / given / chance / voice / second
He ______________________________________

4) He / contract / another / signed / has
He ______________________________________

Looking Back

1. Read the article again. Circle the correct word choice.

Ted Williams, **1) birthday / born** on September 22, 1957, has a **2) God-given / God given** talent of voice; at least that's what the **3) cardbored / cardboard** sign said, as he waited near the road, next to a lane of traffic. Ted was asking for donations. He was homeless, and had been struggling with drug and alcohol addiction for years.

On January 3, 2011, Doral Chenweth, a videographer for the *Columbus Dispatch*, recorded an interview with Ted. During the interview, Ted improvised a professional quality radio advertisement. He had a golden voice; the most **4) soothing / smoothing** and unique baritone voice rolled out of the mouth of a homeless man. Doral knew Ted was special.

During the interview, Ted spoke more about his education and what happened to him, and what events lead up to him becoming homeless. In the video, Ted appeared disheveled, and dirty, but had the voice of an angel.

Doral posted the interview on the Internet, and later it was uploaded to the popular **5) video sharing / video-sharing** site YouTube. By January 5th, Ted was receiving attention **6) by / from** national news and media outlets, pledging interviews, job offers, money and clothes. **7) On / By** the end of the week, Ted was offered jobs from MSNBC, the Cleveland Cavaliers, Kraft Foods, and Quicken Loans Arena.

Although Ted claims to have been sober since mid-2008, he began to drink again **8) before / after** the media attention began. During the month of January 2011, Ted met with popular TV psychologist Phil McGraw, and admitted to drinking alcohol heavily again. He agreed to go to a **9) male-only / only male** drug rehab facility in Texas arranged by Dr. Phil. Ted left the facility after only 12 days. He stated that he desired more anonymity, and that the whole experience felt "scripted." After that, Ted signed reality television deals and book contracts, but in the spring of 2011, Ted yet again returned to an alcohol rehabilitation center. He put his career **10) to / on** hold until he could manage his addiction.

As it **11) stands / stood**, Ted Williams is out of rehab, having finished his program successfully. He has signed another contract to be the official voice of New England Cable News, and works out of his **12) in-home / in home** studio in Dublin, Ohio.

Although Ted will always have to manage his addictions with drugs and alcohol, like other recovering addicts, he has been given a second chance to show the world his God-given talent of voice.

Moral of the story Even if you're down, you're still not out.

2. Answer the following questions related to the story.

1) Can people truly recover from addiction? Why or why not?

2) Why do you think Ted became homeless?

3) Do you think Ted will make good use of his second chance? Do you think people who get second chances often repeat the same mistakes? Why or why not?

Last Chance Glance

Read the job profile below.

Addiction Rehabilitation Social Workers

Addiction rehabilitation social workers can provide individual or group therapy to patients and patient's family members or close friends. They often counsel patients in group homes, residential treatment programs, correctional facilities or hospital treatment programs.

An addiction worker creates records of their patients' history and charts their progress during ongoing sessions. They implement treatment and recovery plans, and perform assessments of their patient's psychological condition. Addictions counselors must ensure that treatment goals are being met, as well as attend staff meetings regarding patient care. They may administer urine samples to determine whether a patient is drug-free.

Addiction workers consult with other professionals in order to assess the physical or mental state of their patients. They must guide their patients in overcoming their addictions and addictive behaviors. Workers may suggest changes in living arrangements to remove their patients from negative environments and influences. Addictions counselors work with their patients in aftercare programs, as well as help them make adjustments without relying on their dependencies.

Requirements for becoming an addiction worker typically vary by country. Sometimes a bachelor's degree or master's degree is required; however, the completion of a certificate program may only be necessary. Potential students should study their country's qualifications for becoming an addictions counselor.

Additionally, individuals who want to become an addictions counselor should possess a caring and compassionate nature. They should be energetic and capable of providing emotional support to their patients.

Answer Key

Chapter 1

c

b

a

a

b

Chapter 2

d

b

c

d

c

Chapter 3

c

d

c

d

c

Chapter 4

c

d

b

c

d

Chapter 5

c

d

b

b

a

Chapter 6

c

d

a

b

a

Chapter 7

d

c

d

a

d

Chapter 8

a

c

a

c

d

Chapter 9

b

c

b

c

d

Chapter 10

c

b

d

a

a

Chapter 11

b

a

c

c

d

Chapter 12

b

a

c

d

c

References

http://www.nypost.com/p/news/national/homeless_man_with_golden_radio_voice_91PQ3yMBa58vOf1n4MuToJ

http://education-portal.com/articles/Addictions_Worker_Job_Description_Duties_and_Requirements.html

http://www.iwillfoundation.com/

http://www.mattslongrun.com/

http://www.runnersworld.com/article/0,7120,s6-243-297--13053-0,00.html

http://culinaryarts.about.com/od/culinaryfundamentals/a/whatisachef.htm

http://edition.cnn.com/2010/LIVING/04/01/cnnheroes.krishnan.hunger/index.html

http://careers.stateuniversity.com/pages/347/Funeral-Director.html

http://www.parrado.com

http://www.globalpost.com/dispatch/news/regions/americas/united-states/111225/jordan-romero-world-climbing-record

http://www.bbc.co.uk/news/world-us-canada-16328714

http://www.jordanromero.com

http://www.theaustralian.com.au/news/lifestyle/teenager-jordan-romero-completes-mountain-climbing-challenge/story-e6frg9zo-1226230513361

http://www.jobdescriptions.net/hospitality/travel-agent/

http://money.usnews.com/money/careers/articles/2010/12/06/best-careers-2011-biomedical-engineer

http://www.worldrecordsacademy.org/youngest/youngest_cancer_researcher_Angela_Zhang_sets_world_record_112634.html

http://www.TaylorMali.com/index.cfm?webid=2

http://www.degreesource.com/articles/178/1/RN-Nursing-Job-Description/Page1.html

http://www.nps.gov/clba/photosmultimedia/Clara-Barton-Photographs.htm

http://careers.stateuniversity.com/pages/483/Optometrist.html

http://www.vdwoxford.org/joshsilver.htm

http://www.guardian.co.uk/society/2008/dec/22/diy-adjustable-glasses-josh-silver

http://www.sportsnet.ca/more/2011/10/24/marathon_no_record/

http://www.bbc.co.uk/news/uk-15370205

http://www.ehow.com/facts_5931137_job-duties-responsibilities-counselor.html

http://www.bbc.co.uk/worldservice/programmes/2011/02/110207_homeless_harvard_liz_murray.shtml

Authors

Myeong-Hee Seong
Ph.D., Korea University
Professor, Eulji University

Katie Mae Klemsen
MA., Monterey Institute of International Studies
Professor, Hanyang University

Tales of Great Feats:
Reading and Writing for English Language Learners

2012년 2월 22일 초판 1쇄 인쇄
2012년 2월 25일 초판 1쇄 발행

공저자 Myeong-Hee Seong
Katie Mae Klemsen
발행인 (寅製) 진 욱 상

저자와의 합의하에 인지첩부 생략

발행처 백산출판사
서울시 성북구 정릉3동 653-40
등 록 : 1974. 1. 9. 제 1-72호
전 화 : 914-1621, 917-6240
FAX : 912-4438
http://www.ibaeksan.kr
editbsp@naver.com

값 12,000원
ISBN 978-89-6183-555-8